The 2000 Presidential Election

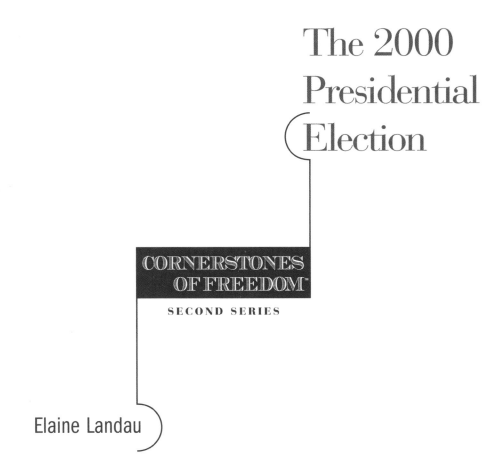

CORNERSTONES OF FREEDOM™

SECOND SERIES

Elaine Landau

Children's Press®
A Division of Scholastic Inc.
New York • Toronto • London • Auckland • Sydney
Mexico City • New Delhi • Hong Kong
Danbury, Connecticut

Photographs © 2002: AP/Wide World Photos: 29 (Charles Rex Arbogast),
17 left (Austin American-Statesman), 31, 45 top (Pat Benic), 12 (Eric Draper),
17 right (James A. Finley), 25, 35 (Mark Foley), 11, 34 (Tony Gutierrez),
27 (Allison Long), 41 (Doug Mills), 30 (Michael Laughlin Pool/Sun Sentinel),
10 top (Ron Thomas); Corbis Images: cover top, 6, 15 (AFP), 39 (Wally
McNamee), cover bottom, 4, 7, 9, 10 bottom, 13, 19, 22, 24, 28 top,
28 bottom, 32, 33, 36, 44 center, 44 top, 45 center (Rueters NewMedia Inc.);
Getty Images: 21 (Tim Boyle/Newsmakers), 3 background, 20 (Stephen
Ferry/Liaison), 18 (Robert King/Newsmakers), 5 (Billy Suratt/Liaison);
Nance S. Trueworthy: 23, 38; PhotoEdit/Billy E. Barnes: 8; Rigoberto
Quinteros: 14, 16, 44 bottom, 45 bottom.

Library of Congress Cataloging-in-Publication Data
Landau, Elaine
  The 2000 Presidential Election / by Elaine Landau.
    p. cm — (Cornerstones of freedom)
  Includes bibliographical references and index.
  Summary: Explores the people and events surrounding the 2000
Presidential Election.
  ISBN 0-516-22527-8 (lib. bdg.)
  1. Presidents—United States—Election—2000—Juvenile literature.
2. Presidential candidates—United States—History—20th century—
Juvenile literature. 3. United States—Politics and government—
1993–2001—Juvenile literature. [1. Presidents—Election—2000.
2. Elections. 3. United States—Politics and government—1993–2001.]
I. Title. II. Series.

  E889 .L36 2002
  324.973'0929—dc21

                          2001006916

CHILDREN'S PRESS, AND CORNERSTONES OF FREEDOM™, and
associated logos are trademarks and or registered trademarks of Grolier
Publishing Co., Inc. SCHOLASTIC and associated logos are trademarks
and or registered trademarks of Scholastic Inc.

1 2 3 4 5 6 7 8 9 10 R 11 10 09 08 07 06 05 04 03 02

EVERY FOUR YEARS IN November, U.S. citizens vote to elect a president. They usually know the name of their next leader before going to bed that night. The 2000 presidential election, however, was a completely different story. It would take more than five weeks of legal battles and protests before a winner was declared. It was an election that the nation and the world would not soon forget.

George W. Bush (left) and Dick Cheney (right) greet reporters outside of the governor's mansion in Austin, Texas.

November 7, 2000, was an exciting day across the United States. Close to 100 million Americans had come to the **polls** on Election Day to elect our forty-third president. Or so they thought.

The presidential candidates ran vigorous campaigns for months before the election, and everyone expected an extremely close race between the Democratic and Republican nominees. Texas Governor George W. Bush ran as the Republican candidate. He was the son of a former U.S. president and had been elected governor of Texas in 1994.

* * * *

At the time of the presidential election, Bush was in his second term as governor. His vice presidential running mate was Dick Cheney. Cheney had been secretary of defense when Bush's father was president.

The Democratic Party's nominee, Albert A. Gore, Jr. was serving his second term as vice president under President Bill Clinton. Gore formerly had been a congressman and an influential U.S. senator. Like George W. Bush, he came from a political family. Gore's father had been a U.S. senator. Gore's running mate was Senator Joseph Lieberman of Connecticut. Senator Lieberman was the first Jewish candidate for vice president.

WOULD HISTORY REPEAT ITSELF?

On election night the country wondered if George W. Bush would follow in his father's footsteps. The only other father and son to be elected president of the United States were John Adams in 1796 and John Quincy Adams in 1825.

Al Gore (left) and Joseph Lieberman (right) wave to the crowd at Tennessee State University during a campaign stop.

Two other presidential candidates influenced the election—Ralph Nader and Pat Buchanan. Ralph Nader ran as the **Green Party**'s candidate. His views were closer to Al Gore's than to George W. Bush's. Therefore, some people believed that votes cast for Nader would hurt Gore's chances of winning. Pat Buchanan, the **Reform Party**'s candidate, was also on the ballot. Buchanan was the most conservative candidate. Both Nader and Buchanan received very small percentages of the total national vote. Nevertheless, in this amazingly close race, even these small percentages made an important difference.

Pat Buchanan (left), the Reform Party candidate, shakes hands with Ralph Nader (right), the Green Party candidate, at a press conference.

The polls were crowded on Election Day. This photograph shows people waiting in line to vote in a public school gym in Brooklyn, New York.

VOTERS CROWD THE POLLS

The polling places were busy on Election Day, with a number of states reporting having long lines at the polls. As in many previous close elections, the Republican and Democratic parties actively encouraged people to vote. They telephoned voters urging them to cast their ballots. Sometimes they even arranged for transportation to voting places for those who had none. Religious groups, unions, and other organizations also appealed to people to make their voices heard in the election.

7

ARE EXIT POLLS ALWAYS ACCURATE?

Most national exit polls have a built-in sampling error, which is the range of percentage points allowed for error above and below a certain number. But this assumes both that scientific procedures were followed in selecting the people polled and that a large enough number of people were polled. Either of these factors can affect a poll's accuracy.

A woman interviews a voter in election exit poll. Exit pollsters wait for people to leave the polling places to ask them about who they voted for in the election.

Polls showed Bush leading Gore by a slight margin a few weeks before the election. Gore campaigned hard and soon made up the difference, so that by Election Day the contest was too close to call.

On election night millions of Americans watched the election results on television. Everyone thought that they would know who our new president was before going to bed. That's because for many years the news networks **projected**, or "called," elections before all the votes were counted. They made their calls based on **exit polls** and early returns. People conduct exit polls by asking a sample of voters who they voted for as they leave the polls. Early returns come from voting places that have closed and already counted their votes.

Usually, the sample surveyed reflects how the nation will vote. However, in a very close election there is less room for error, and so the sample may not give an accurate reading. There was yet another problem with the national exit poll. To save money, only one company, Voters News Service, was hired to conduct the poll. Therefore, if there was an error in the poll, every news service and network throughout the country would report the same wrong information. Yet, as the polls were beginning to close that night, few people were thinking about errors. The nation only wanted results. As it turned out, however, it would have to wait a long time.

ELECTING THE ELECTORS

Many voters believe they are electing the president when they are casting their ballots. Actually, they are only voting for electors pledged to support one presidential candidate. As a group these electors are known as the Electoral College.

Electoral College delegate Barbara Lett Simmons from Washington, D.C., signs papers certifying her vote in the 2000 presidential election.

ELECTORAL COLLEGE— SHOULD IT GO OR STAY?

The Electoral College is often criticized. Since our nation's birth, Congress has seen more than seven hundred proposals to either change or do away with it. Nevertheless, this system still has its share of supporters.

9

Two young people who work for the House of Representatives carry the boxes containing the votes of the Electoral College to a congressional session. It is part of the vice president's job to certify the votes of the Electoral College for president.

★ ★ ★ ★

The number of electoral votes each state has is equal to the number of representatives it sends to the House of Representatives and the number of senators it sends to the Senate. Each state has two senators, but the number of its representatives is based on the size of the population of the state. Therefore, more heavily populated states, such as California, have more electoral votes than less populated states, such as Wyoming. Candidates fight hard to win the more populated states.

In the 2000 election, both political parties paid close attention to several key states. These states had a high number of electoral votes and could have gone for either candidate. Because they could sway the election, they were called **swing states**. Swing states in the 2000 election included Michigan, Pennsylvania, and Florida. Both Bush and Gore had campaigned heavily in all of these states—especially Florida.

Al Gore interacts with a crowd of his supporters gathered for a political rally in South Beach, Florida.

10

George W. Bush addresses supporters at Palm Beach International Airport. His brother, Jeb, stands behind him on the left.

BUSH'S LITTLE BROTHER

Jeb Bush, who was born on February 11, 1953, is George W. Bush's younger brother. Jeb Bush moved to Florida in 1980 where he helped start an impressive real estate company. While in the Sunshine State, he became active in politics. In 1998 he ran successfully for governor of Florida.

CANDIDATES BATTLE FOR FLORIDA—THE SUNSHINE STATE

Some people felt that Governor Bush had an advantage in Florida because the state's Republican governor was Bush's younger brother, Jeb Bush. Yet Florida also had a number of strongly Democratic counties in which Gore had spent a good deal of time and money. He also strongly campaigned in minority group neighborhoods. His efforts paid off. Minority group voters in Florida went to the polls in record numbers.

11

George W. Bush talks on the telephone while watching the election results with his family. His father, former President George Bush, sits beside him. His mother, Barbara, can be seen in the background.

Gore received a boost at 7:49 P.M., eastern standard time (EST), when the news services started projecting him as the winner in Florida. That call was a serious blow to the Bush campaign. The entire Bush family had been watching the election returns in a private dining room in a Texas hotel. They had been in a wonderfully festive mood, speaking of a future in the White House while dining on fried chicken, shrimp, and ice cream. But the Florida projections suddenly ended the Bush family party. The family headed back to the governor's mansion where they could be in closer touch with campaign headquarters.

★ ★ ★ ★

Al Gore campaigned hard to win key states, such as Michigan. This photograph was taken a rally at the University of Michigan a few days before the election.

The news from Florida distressed Bush campaigners because the news services had made their projection before the polls in the Florida panhandle were closed. The panhandle region is in the central standard time (CST) zone, where it is an hour earlier than in the rest of the state, which is in the eastern standard time zone. The panhandle usually voted Republican. Now Bush supporters feared that voters there might not feel their votes mattered. If they failed to cast their ballots, Bush's chances could be hurt.

Next, Gore was declared a winner in Michigan. Then just after 9:00 P.M. the networks reported that Gore had won in

Pennsylvania, too. Gore was now the projected winner in three swing states. As their sizable electoral votes were **tallied**, it seemed that the nation's vice president might soon be its new president.

Al Gore listened to the election returns from his hotel room in Nashville, Tennessee. The vice president was delighted by the recent gains but continued campaigning. Aware that polls were still open in the West, he called key radio stations there. It was his last chance to urge voters to cast their ballots for him.

As it turned out, Vice President Al Gore needed all the help he could get. Later election returns showed that the network's earlier Florida call for Gore was wrong. Votes for Bush were beginning to add up, seriously challenging Gore's lead.

Then just before 10:00 P.M. the networks took back their earlier prediction. The election in Florida, they now said, was too close to call. One anchorperson noted, "The networks giveth and the networks taketh away."

As the hours passed, the votes continued to be counted. It soon became obvious that neither Gore nor Bush could win the presidency without Florida. The state's twenty-five electoral votes had become more **crucial** than ever.

When the clock struck midnight, Americans still didn't know who their next president would be. At 1:00 A.M.

Governor Bush had a lead of 250,000 votes in Florida. Yet there were some largely Democratic counties whose votes still hadn't been counted. Nevertheless, by 2:00 A.M. Bush was believed to be far in the lead. At 2:16 A.M. the networks began making the most critical call of the election. They projected that George W. Bush had won Florida and therefore the presidency. Vice President Gore called Governor Bush to **concede** the election and congratulate him.

It was a jubilant time in Austin, Texas. The crowd of about eight thousand Bush supporters outside the state house cheered. Red, white, and blue floodlights were flashed on the building, and the celebrating started. It was raining, but that didn't seem to dampen the crowd's enthusiasm. Everyone there was anxious for Bush to declare victory.

Within the hour, however, things began to turn around again. It appeared that the networks might have made a second serious error. Bush's lead in Florida was beginning to slip. Vice President Gore was informed of the dwindling vote margin. He received the call on a cell phone while riding in a motorcade en route to making his concession speech.

Bush supporters flooded the streets around the State of Texas Capitol Building in Austin, Texas, to celebrate Bush's victory on election night.

CONTINUED PEACE & PROSPERITY
PRESIDENT
VICE PRESIDENT
AL GORE
JOE LIEBERMAN

Now Gore's campaign advisors urged him not to give up yet. Bush's lead had dropped to just hundreds of votes out of more than 6 million votes cast in Florida. Obviously, the race wasn't over yet. According to Florida law, when an election margin falls below one-half of 1 percent, the state automatically requires a recount.

THE PRESIDENTIAL RACE CONTINUES

Vice President Gore decided to remain in the race. At about 3:15 A.M. he called Governor Bush and withdrew his concession. Al Gore was not the only one taking things back. The news networks began to realize that they had made another major error. At nearly the same time they all took back their projection that Bush had won the election. Once again Florida was considered too close to call.

Still, some election results were clear. Bush had carried the South, the Rocky Mountain states, and most of the Plains states. Gore won New York and California, along with the Northeast and much of the Great Lakes region.

Al Gore won the national popular vote. He actually received more votes than George W. Bush. But because of the Electoral College, a presidential candidate may win more votes than his opponent and still lose the election. In

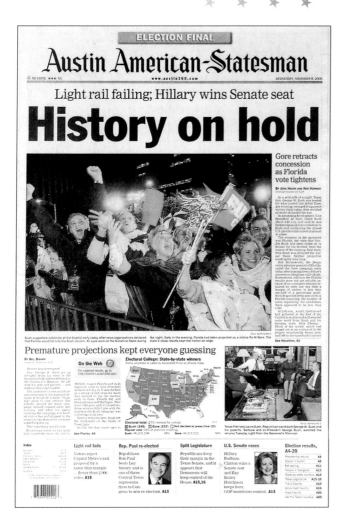

This Austin newspaper first reported that Bush had won. Then, in later editions, they declared the election too close to call.

This newspaper headline reflects the mood of the nation after the election.

our system, electoral votes are what counts. To win the election, a candidate must have 270 electoral votes to have a majority of the votes of the Electoral College. As of November 8, Al Gore had 262 electoral votes and George W. Bush had 246 electoral votes, excluding Florida's electoral votes.

Therefore, the next president of the United States would be
the candidate who won Florida—and its crucial twenty-five
electoral votes. Americans, along with people everywhere,
would have to wait until the votes were counted there. The
eyes of the world turned to Florida.

Anyone who thought the campaign ended on Election
Day was wrong. Both the Bush and Gore teams became
active in Florida arguing their case. George W. Bush took
the position that he was the winner and that the automatic state recount was merely a standard requirement.
He remained in Texas, where he began to put together a
cabinet for his presidency. Al Gore, on the other hand,
championed the cause of ensuring that the people's will
was done. He argued that the only way to do that was
through an accurate recount.

Bush dispatched former Secretary of State James Baker to Florida. Baker, a loyal Republican and a good friend of former President Bush, was sent there to look out for George W. Bush's interests. For his part, Gore asked Democrat Warren Christopher, another former secretary of state, to represent him in Florida. Both of these statesmen would work vigorously to sway public opinion in their candidate's favor.

Baker and Bush's Florida team insisted that Bush had won in polling booths throughout Florida while Warren Christopher and Gore's team maintained that a recount

SPEAKING FOR THE DEMOCRATS

Democrat Warren Christopher had a distinguished career in government. He served as secretary of state under President Bill Clinton and at different times had been actively involved in working on Arab-Israeli peace agreements.

On November 11, after meeting with Gore, Warren Christopher tells members of the news media about Gore's position on the Florida recount. William Daley, chairman of the Gore campaign, stands alongside Christopher.

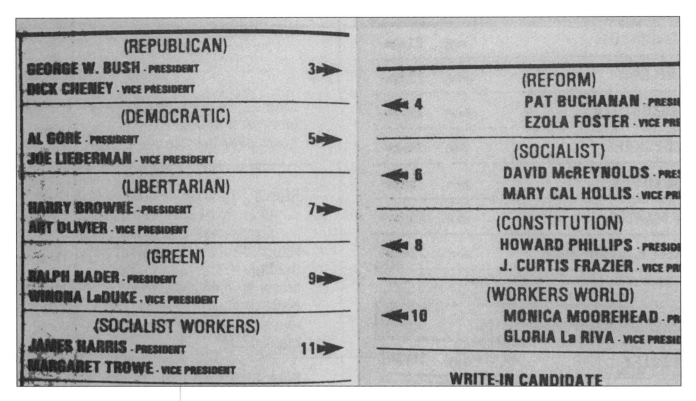

(REPUBLICAN)
GEORGE W. BUSH - PRESIDENT   3➤
DICK CHENEY - VICE PRESIDENT

(DEMOCRATIC)
AL GORE - PRESIDENT   5➤
JOE LIEBERMAN - VICE PRESIDENT

(LIBERTARIAN)
HARRY BROWNE - PRESIDENT   7➤
ART OLIVIER - VICE PRESIDENT

(GREEN)
RALPH NADER - PRESIDENT   9➤
WINONA LaDUKE - VICE PRESIDENT

(SOCIALIST WORKERS)
JAMES HARRIS - PRESIDENT   11➤
MARGARET TROWE - VICE PRESIDENT

◄ 4   (REFORM)
        PAT BUCHANAN - PRESI
        EZOLA FOSTER - VICE PRI

◄ 6   (SOCIALIST)
        DAVID McREYNOLDS - PRES
        MARY CAL HOLLIS - VICE PRI

◄ 8   (CONSTITUTION)
        HOWARD PHILLIPS - PRESIDI
        J. CURTIS FRAZIER - VICE PRI

◄ 10   (WORKERS WORLD)
        MONICA MOOREHEAD - PR
        GLORIA La RIVA - VICE PRESI

        WRITE-IN CANDIDATE

This is a close-up photograph of a butterfly ballot.

would show Gore as the true winner in Florida. He had won the nation's popular vote and they wanted the public to see Gore as the people's true choice.

Early on, problems in Florida's Palm Beach County surfaced. A new type of ballot used there was supposed to make voting easier for older citizens. Known as the **butterfly ballot**, it looked like an open book. The nominees' names were on opposite sides with punch holes down the center.

A large number of voters were confused by the way the candidates' names appeared. Many Gore supporters, for example, accidentally voted for Pat Buchanan because his

* * * *

name was printed across from Gore's on the ballot. Some who realized their mistake tried to remedy it by punching the ballot again for Gore. More than nineteen thousand of these **double-punched ballots** were declared invalid and so were not counted. Another ten thousand ballots came in with the presidential line left blank. Because of the large number of Democratic voters in Palm Beach County, these were viewed as lost votes for Al Gore.

There were voting difficulties in other parts of the state, too. Mechanical vote counts are never entirely accurate and usually this doesn't change an election's results. In a very close race, however, a small number of miscounted ballots can make a difference. The Gore team argued that Florida's automatic machine recount would miss partially punched ballots. They insisted that only a hand count would show the voter's "clear intent."

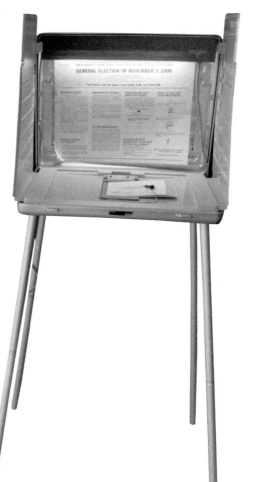

County election canvassing boards oversee and **certify** election results in their counties. Under Florida law, the boards can conduct hand counts. At the Democrats' request hand counts were eventually begun in four Florida counties—which were largely Democratic areas.

The Republicans pursued a different strategy, maintaining that George Bush had won on the first ballot count and the machine recount. They insisted that hand counts were less reliable than machine tallies. Human counting, they said, was subject to both errors and mischief.

Disagreement also arose over which ballots were valid. People argued over counting ballots in which the **chad**—the part of the ballot that voters punch out—was just partly punched out or indented. The Republicans further complained that

A protester holds a copy of the disputed butterfly ballot outside the Palm Beach County Courthouse on November 9.

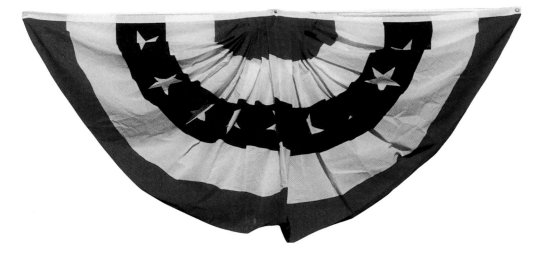

there were no statewide standards to guide the people who were doing the counting. Therefore, a ballot that was counted in one county might be discarded in the next.

Meanwhile, Florida took on a carnival-like atmosphere. Large numbers of lawyers, journalists, and politicians flocked to the Sunshine State, and protests were held in the streets over voting irregularities. Demonstrators carried signs protesting confusing ballots. One sign read, "High-Tech America, Low-Tech Voting System."

The Republicans accused the Democrats of dragging out the election to get a favorable outcome. They claimed that the stock market was suffering because of all the indecision. The Democrats countered that the disputed election had not put the nation in crisis. What really mattered, they said, was an accurate count. Gore's team continually repeated that speed was less important than carrying out the will of the people. The Republicans fought this assertion at every turn. And both sides found experts to back their different viewpoints.

Theodore Olson, an attorney for Bush, answers questions from reporters after a Miami judge refused Bush's request to stop the manual recount on November 13.

LEGAL BATTLES OVER THE FLORIDA ELECTION

Voters from Palm Beach County went to court over the confusing ballots. Others sued claiming that they had not had enough time at their polling places. Still other suits accused highway patrol officers of discouraging African Americans from voting by setting up vehicle checkpoints near polling places. African Americans also sued over other voting irregularities. After arriving at the polls, many had been told that they were not registered to vote.

Democratic voters in Martin and Seminole counties brought additional suits to challenge the validity of **absentee ballots** there. In one suit, lawyers argued that election officials had allowed Republicans to add voter identification numbers that had been left off the absentee ballot applications due to a printing error. Since these absentee ballots were believed to be largely from Republican voters, counting them would strengthen Bush's position in the race.

Both the Gore and Bush teams were busy in the courts as well. Bush's group went to federal court on November 12 to block the hand counts but was defeated. Yet to the Republicans' advantage, Florida Secretary of State Katherine Harris announced that she would enforce the

Florida Secretary of State Katherine Harris denied attempts by some Florida counties to extend the deadline.

FLORIDA'S SECRETARY OF STATE

Katherine Harris comes from a highly respected Florida

family. Her grandfather served in the Florida legislature.

Harris graduated from Agnes Scott College and went

on to earn a master's degree at Harvard University.

Before becoming active in politics, she was a

commercial real estate broker.

November 14 deadline for county vote tallies set by the Florida legislature. Only absentee ballots due by November 17, she declared, would be added to these totals.

This deadline left no time to complete the hand counts. When three counties requested an extension, Harris refused to budge. "The reasons given in the requests are insufficient to warrant a waiver of the **unambiguous** filing deadline," she explained.

Katherine Harris, a Republican, had been cochairperson of Bush's Florida campaign. The Democrats, believing her actions were designed to put Bush in the White House, fought her decision in court. After a lower court supported Harris, the case was taken to Florida's Supreme Court.

THE FLORIDA SUPREME COURT GIVES GORE MORE TIME

On November 17, the Florida Supreme Court prohibited Harris from immediately certifying the election results. It later ruled that hand counts would be included in the final election tallies. The court set a new deadline of November 26 for the hand count totals to be in. This decision was a victory for Gore.

Bush believed that the Florida Supreme Court had overstepped its bounds in extending the deadline. Bush asked the U.S. Supreme Court, the highest court in the land, to hear the case. After reviewing it, the U.S. Supreme Court set aside the Florida Supreme Court's ruling and asked the Florida Supreme Court to provide more information on how it arrived at its decision.

Attorney Paul Hancock (standing) from the Florida State Attorney General's office is questioned by Chief Justice Charles Wells (center) during a hearing on Harris's decision to certify the Florida vote.

But at that point Governor Bush had something else to be concerned about. On November 22, his running mate, Dick Cheney, had suffered a mild heart attack. Cheney was soon released from the hospital. Cheney had a history of heart trouble, and some voters began to wonder about his ability to serve.

CANDIDATE FOR VICE PRESIDENT

Dick Cheney brought a wealth of political experience to the Bush team. He had been a White House official, a congressman, and a cabinet official. Cheney had been widely praised for his handling of the Gulf War in 1991 under former President Bush. He was the secretary of defense at the time.

27

Katherine Harris signs the documents to certify the Florida vote on November 26.

Bush asks Gore to reconsider his court challenges after the Florida vote was certified. He said that he was preparing to serve as the next president of the United States.

Meanwhile, on November 26, the new deadline for the hand count tallies, Governor Bush was still slightly ahead. Katherine Harris certified the votes and declared him the winner in Florida. That brought Bush's total of electoral votes to 271—one more than was needed to win the presidency. Bush had won Florida by less than one-half of one-thousandth of 1 percent.

George W. Bush claimed that he was now the president-elect and publicly asked Gore to concede. "Now that the votes are counted, it's time for the votes to count," the then Texas governor told the nation. But Gore's team argued that Bush had not won at all. They believed that the vote tallies were inaccurate. Democrats stressed that Miami-Dade County had not had time to do the hand recount. They said that election officials there stopped counting after being intimidated by rowdy Republican demonstrators who had been bused in.

Palm Beach County election officials had worked through the night in the recount but had not finished. The Palm Beach counters needed just two more hours, but Secretary Harris refused to extend the deadline. She also refused to accept the numbers from their partial hand recount.

The Democrats had yet another objection, which they called the Thanksgiving Surprise. Over the holiday Nassau County had discovered a large number of extra ballots for Bush. The Democrats found this suspicious. For all these reasons and others, they headed off to court.

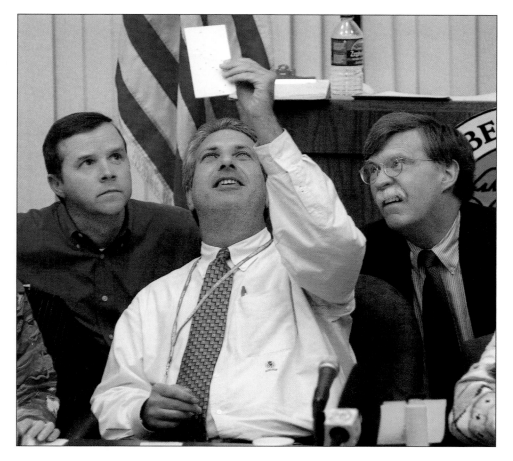

A lawyer from each side of the voting controversy looks on as Judge Charles Burton, chair of the Palm Beach County canvassing board, holds up the last ballot to be counted in the manual recount. Officials stopped their recount with as many as 1,000 questionable ballots left to check.

BOTH SIDES HEAD BACK TO COURT

Gore's lawyers wanted Katherine Harris's certified election results overturned. They asked a state circuit court to order a hand count of about thirteen thousand ballots in Miami-Dade and Palm Beach counties. These ballots were **undervotes,** which means that previous machine counts of these ballots had shown no vote for president.

29

On December 4, Florida Circuit Court Judge N. Sanders Sauls ruled against Gore. The vice president's legal team appealed the case in Florida's Supreme Court. On December 8, the Florida Supreme Court reversed the lower court's decision. The court went further than just ruling that the undervotes in select counties be counted. To be fair to all voters, the court ordered a hand recount of the undervotes in all Florida counties in which such a count was not previously done.

That ruling would be Gore's last victory. The hand counts began after the court decision, but after Bush's attorneys asked the U.S. Supreme Court to halt them the recounts were stopped on December 9. On December 12, the court ruled that the recounts had not been constitutional.

Judge N. Sanders Sauls listens to attorneys from both sides about whether to overturn the state certification of Bush as the winner of the election.

Supporters of both candidates protest in front of the Supreme Court.

The majority of judges on the court reasoned that because different standards had been used to count the votes in various counties, these recounts violated the equal protection clause of the U.S. Constitution's Fourteenth Amendment.

The U.S. Supreme Court said that the recounts could continue if uniform standards were set. But in the same decision it indicated that there was not enough time for that. Gore only had until December 12—the date the Florida legislature was scheduled to submit its slate of presidential electors to the Electoral College. If things weren't settled by then, the state legislature was prepared to step in. The legislature had already called a

THE EQUAL PROTECTION CLAUSE

The equal protection clause of the Fourteenth Amendment guarantees that a state's laws will be applied to everyone in the same way. Questions of whether the equal protection clause has been violated arise when one group of individuals is granted the right to engage in an activity while others are denied the same right.

Florida House and Senate representatives listen to lawyer Thomas Julin give them advice about the Florida election results.

special session to pick their own presidential electors. Since the legislature had a Republican majority, some complained that this was a political back-up plan for George W. Bush. But the Republicans stressed that it was necessary to ensure that Florida voters were represented in the Electoral College.

BUSH DECLARED THE WINNER

The U.S. Supreme Court ruled against Gore's team just hours before the December 12 midnight deadline. By the early hours of the morning, the vice president's political advisors confirmed what he already suspected—it was over. To take the case further seemed pointless.

Al Gore had previously said that he would abide by the U.S. Supreme Court's ruling. Therefore, on December 13 he conceded, noting, "Now the Supreme Court has spoken. . . .

While I strongly disagree with the Court's position, I accept it." Some Democrats believed that the Republican majority on the U.S. Supreme Court had ruled along political party lines. Many Republicans had said the same thing about the mostly Democratic judges on the Florida Supreme Court.

It was a difficult time. Gore and his supporters thought they had won, and the Bush team thought they were victorious. As things stood, the election was close to being a tie. Gore had more of the popular vote—50,996,582 votes to Bush's 50,456,062 votes. However, with the 25 electoral votes from Florida, Bush had the necessary majority of the electoral votes—271 votes to Gore's 262 votes. Gore was the first presidential candidate to win the popular vote and lose the presidency in more than one hundred years. The previous presidential candidate to win the popular vote and lose the election was Grover Cleveland in 1888. The

Democrats wondered what would have happened if there had been time to finish the hand recount. The Republicans insisted that no hand count would ever be accurate without uniform standards.

Through it all, George W. Bush tried to be a gracious winner. He held no lavish victory celebrations and simply urged all Americans to "put politics behind us and work together." Shortly after Gore withdrew from the presidential race, Bush addressed the United States for the first time as president-elect. "I was not elected to serve one party, but to serve one nation," he told the American people. "The President of the United States is the president of every single American, of every race and every background. Whether you voted for me or not, I will do my best to serve your interests, and I will work to earn your respect."

A newspaper designer works on the front page of a Florida newspaper. The outcome of the Florida elections has finally been reached.

A representative of a technology company shows members of Florida's Select Task Force on Election, Procedures and Technology a new computerized voting machine.

Achieving unity would be crucial to the success of his presidency. There had only been three other U.S. presidents before Bush who had won the electoral vote but lost the popular vote. And all three had been one-term presidents.

The presidential election of 2000 was probably the closest and most **turbulent** presidential contest in modern U.S. history. It took thirty-six days before Americans and the rest of the world knew who the forty-third president of the United States would be. Its outcome also encouraged some people to work to change how elections would be conducted in the future. On May 4, 2001, Florida legislators approved a sweeping election reform bill. Among other changes, the bill banned punch card voting systems in Florida. In the

ELECTORAL COLLEGE WINNERS

Former presidents John Quincy Adams, Benjamin Harrison, and Rutherford B. Hayes had all lost the popular vote but won the presidency in the Electoral College. In 2000, George W. Bush became the first president in 112 years to do the same.

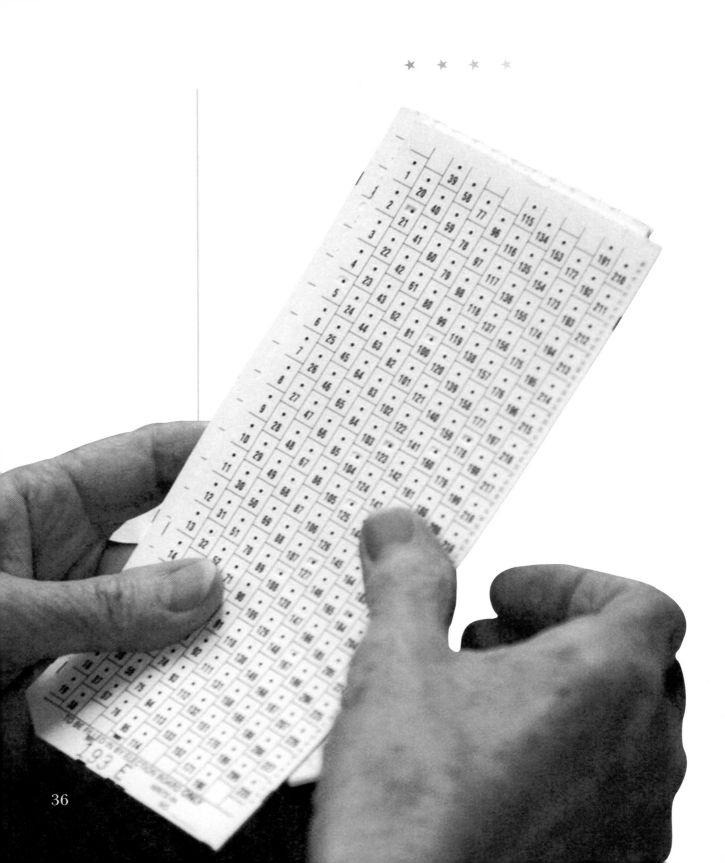

future all counties would be required to use electronic or other vote tabulation systems. The state also developed uniform polling place procedures to ensure that voters would be treated fairly throughout the state. Following the 2000 presidential election, other states began looking into election reform measures as well.

Many of the problems that surfaced had occurred in previous elections, but they had not been important because none of the races had been as close as the 2000 election. Americans wanted to make sure these problems would never happen again. As a result, task forces were set up to examine election standards and voting methods.

Investigations were made into possible voting rights violations affecting minorities. These inquiries yielded some unsettling results. A report by the U.S. Commission on Civil Rights indicated that in the 2000 presidential election, African Americans in Florida had been nine times more likely than whites to have their ballots rejected during the counting process. The report further noted that faulty voting systems had been most common in districts where there were minority voters.

Much of the blame for the voting problems rested with state and county officials. The report described them as failing "to fulfill their duties" in a number of ways. Among those cited for not doing all they could to remedy the problems were Florida Secretary of State Katherine Harris and Florida Governor Jeb Bush.

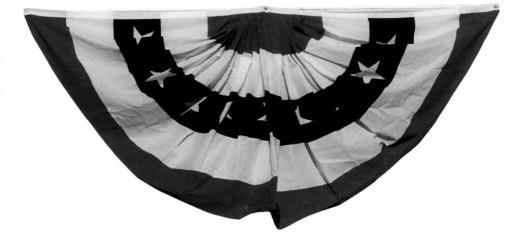

These findings were later confirmed in a report compiled by a commission of election administrators. Their investigation was sponsored by the Election Center, a nonpartisan, nonprofit center that assists election officials. The commission's report called for a federal investigation. It also made the following recommendations:

Rules for holding recounts must be uniform throughout the state.

Media sources should not project election night results before 11 P.M. eastern standard time.

Laws should not be made standardizing poll hours throughout the nation. This could cause hardships in some areas.

Congress should consider making Election Day a national holiday.

Poll workers should be trained to be sensitive to race, ethnic background, and disabilities.

* * * *

The 2000 presidential election sparked a great deal of controversy. However, many people are hopeful that bringing these problems to light will result in necessary changes. Perhaps most importantly, the election provided a reassuring test of our democracy. As Supreme Court Chief Justice William Rehnquist noted in his year-end report to Congress—"This presidential election…tested our…constitutional system in

William Rehnquist was appointed to the Supreme Court by President Richard Nixon in 1971. He became the chief justice in 1986.

ways it has never been tested before. The…courts… became involved in a way that one hopes will seldom, if ever, be necessary in the future."

Politically, the nation was divided. Neither side had wanted to give up, for both believed they were right. In countries without our democratic traditions, there might have been tanks in the streets and martial law. But that's not the American way.

Vice President Al Gore underscored our country's real strength in his concession speech. He urged his supporters to unite behind George W. Bush, saying: "We close ranks when the contest is done…. What remains of partisan rancor must now be put aside and may God bless his [Bush's] stewardship of this country."

George W. Bush was sworn in as the forty-third president of the United States of America on January 20, 2001. It was a cold rainy day with temperatures dipping into the low 30s. Yet hundreds of thousands of people still gathered on the grounds of the Capitol Building and the western portions of the National Mall to witness this historic event.

Bush's inaugural address was brief, clocking in at just under 15 minutes. During the address, the President asked his fellow Americans to "be citizens, not spectators; citizens, not subjects; responsible citizens, building communities of service and a nation of character." That day the President made no reference to the Florida ballot battle that led to his belated presidential victory. Instead he thanked Al Gore for an election campaign that was "conducted in spirit and ended in grace."

President Bush and First Lady Laura Bush walk down Pennsylvania Avenue in Washington, D.C., shortly after George W. Bush was sworn in as the forty-third president of the United States.

The swearing-in ceremony finalized the election results in the minds of people everywhere. One of the most hotly debated presidential elections in our nation's history was finally over. Now it is up to all Americans and their elected officials to make sure our electoral process improves because of those unforgettable thirty-six days in Florida.

41

Glossary

absentee ballot—a ballot sent in by a voter who cannot be at the polls on Election Day

butterfly ballot—a ballot that looks like an open book. The nominees' names are on opposite sides with the punch holes down the center.

certify—to officially guarantee something to be true

chad—the part of the ballot the voter punches out

concede—to give up

crucial—extremely important

double-punched ballot—a ballot in which the voter accidentally voted for two different candidates for the same office

exit poll—a survey of a sample of voters just after they cast their ballot to find out how they voted

Green Party—a political party that supports nonviolence, environmental awareness, and social justice

polls—the places where votes are cast or recorded

projected—to look ahead or to forecast

Reform Party—a political party that wants to change the U.S. political and taxation systems

swing states—states with a high number of electoral votes that could sway an election

tallied—added up or counted

turbulent—wild or confused

unambiguous—clear or certain

undervotes—votes not counted in a machine tally

Timeline: 2000

NOVEMBER 7
Voters go to the polls to elect the forty-third U.S. president on Election Day.

NOVEMBER 8
News media declares Bush the winner at around 2:16 A.M. and Gore concedes to Bush. Gore calls Bush back an hour later and withdraws his concession of the election.

NOVEMBER 9
Former Secretary of State James Baker goes to Florida and speaks to the press about Bush's position on the Florida recount.

NOVEMBER 11
Former Secretary of State Warren Christopher meets with Vice President Al Gore in Washington, D.C., and discusses Gore's position on the recount.

NOVEMBER 12
George W. Bush's lawyers go to federal court to stop the hand counts. They are defeated.

NOVEMBER 14
The Florida legislature establishes this date as the filing deadline for counties to report election results.

NOVEMBER 17
The Florida Supreme Court prohibits Katherine Harris from certifying Florida's presidential election results.

44

Presidential Election

NOVEMBER 21
The Florida Supreme Court orders hand counting of votes to continue and extends the deadline to November 26.

NOVEMBER 26
Katherine Harris certifies the votes and declares Bush the winner in Florida.

DECEMBER 4
The Florida Circuit Court rules against Gore.

DECEMBER 8
The Florida Supreme Court orders a manual recount of the undervotes in all Florida counties where a recount has not already been done.

DECEMBER 9
The U.S. Supreme Court orders the manual recount of undervotes stopped.

DECEMBER 12
The U.S. Supreme Court rules that the manual recounts are un-constitutional.

DECEMBER 13
Al Gore concedes.

45

To Find Out More

BOOKS

Andryszewski, Tricia. *The Reform Party: Ross Perot and Pat Buchanan.*New Milford, CT: Millbrook Press, 2000.

Greenberg, Judith E. *Young People's Letters to the President.* Danbury, CT: Franklin Watts, 1998.

Quiri, Patricia Ryon. *The Supreme Court.* Danbury, CT: Children's Press, 1999.

Robb, Dan. *Hail to the Chief.* Watertown, MA: Charlesbridge, 2000.

St. George, Judith. *So You Want to Be President.* New York: Philomel Books, 2000.

Schaefer, Lola M. *Pledge of Allegiance.* Chicago: Heinemann Library, 2001.

ORGANIZATIONS AND ONLINE SITES

The American Presidency
http://gi.grolier.com/presidents/preshome.html

Mr. President: Profiles of Our Nation's Leaders
http://educate.si.edu/president/gallery/main.cfm

The White House
http://www.whitehousekids.gov

Index

Bold numbers indicate illustrations.

Absentee ballots, 25, 26

Baker, James, **18**, 19–20

Buchannan, Pat, 6, **6**, 20–21

Bush, George W., 4–5, **4**, **11**, **12**, **14**, 15, 18, 19, **28**, 34, 40, **41**

Bush, Jeb, 11, **11**, 37

butterfly ballot, 20–21, **20**, 22

Chads, 22

Cheney, Dick, **4**, 5, **14**, 27

Christopher, Warren, 19–20, 19

Democratic Party, 5, 7, 23, 33, 34

double-punched ballots, 21

Electoral College, 9–10, **9**, **10**, 16, 17, 31, 32, 35

electoral votes, 10, 17–18, 28, 33

exit polls, 8–9, **8**

Florida, 11, 12, 13, 14, 15, 16, 18, 23, 25, 28

election reform, 35, **35**, 37

Miami-Dade County, 28, 29

Palm Beach County, 20, 21, 24, 29

state legislature, 31–32, **32**

Supreme Court, 26, **27**, 30, 33

Gore, Al, 5, **5**, **10**, 12, 13–14, **13**, 15, **16**, 18, 32–33, **33**, 40

Hancock, Paul, **27**

Harris, Katherine, 25–26, **25**, 28, **28**, 29, 37

Lieberman, Joseph, 5, **5**, **16**, 33

Minority voters, 11, 24, 37

Nader, Ralph, 6, **6**

Polls, 4, 7, **7**

popular vote, 16, 33

Recount, 16, 18, 19–20, 21, 22–23, 26, 28, 29, **29**, 30, 34

Rehnquist, William, 39–40

Republican Party, 4, 7, 22–23, 33

Sauls, N. Sanders, 30, **30**

swing states, 10

U.S. Supreme Court, 26, 30–31, **31**, 32–33, 39

undervotes, 29, 30

About the Author

Popular author **Elaine Landau** worked as a newspaper reporter, editor, and as a youth services librarian before becoming a full-time writer. She has written more than 185 nonfiction books for young people. Ms. Landau, who has a bachelor's degree in English and journalism from New York University and a master's degree in library and information science from Pratt Institute, lives in Miami, Florida, with her husband and son.